Girlfriend to Girlfriend

Girlfriend to

Julia A. Boyd

Girlfriend

Everyday Wisdom and
Affirmations from the
Sister Circle

A DUTTON BOOK

DUTTON
Published by the Penguin Group
Penguin Books USA Inc., 375 Hudson Street,
New York, New York 10014, U.S.A.
Penguin Books Ltd, 27 Wrights Lane, London W8 5TZ, England
Penguin Books Australia Ltd, Ringwood, Victoria, Australia
Penguin Books Canada Ltd, 10 Alcorn Avenue,
Toronto, Ontario, Canada M4V 3B2
Penguin Books (N.Z.) Ltd, 182–190 Wairau Road,
Auckland 10, New Zealand

Penguin Books Ltd, Registered Offices: Harmondsworth, Middlesex, England

First published by Dutton, an imprint of Dutton Signet,
a division of Penguin Books USA Inc.
Distributed in Canada by McClelland & Stewart Inc.

First Printing, May, 1995
10 9 8 7 6 5 4 3 2 1

 REGISTERED TRADEMARK—MARCA REGISTRADA

LIBRARY OF CONGRESS CATALOGING-IN-PUBLICATION DATA:
Boyd, Julia A.
   Girlfriend to girlfriend : everyday wisdom and affirmations from the sister circle
/ Julia Boyd.
      p.   cm.
   ISBN 0-525-93958-X
   1. Afro-American women—Life skills guides. 2. Afro-American women—
Psychology. 3. Afro-American women—Quotations. I. Title.
E185.86.B646   1995
305.48'896073—dc20   94-43086
                                                               CIP

Printed in the United States of America
Set in Goudy Old Style
Designed by Eve L. Kirch

This book is printed on acid-free paper.

To my parents,
Lavada and Joseph Conyers,
with all my love

Contents

Acknowledgments

I would like to send a very special thank you to all of the girlfriends who have welcomed and supported me throughout my travels in the past year. In our short times together we've shared laughter, wisdom, and just good old homegirl times, and my memories of those times are some of my greatest treasures. I would like to thank my family, the Conyers, Dunns, and Boyds, for your love, support, and encouragement—I'm truly blessed to have you all in my life. To my agent, Elizabeth Wales, and her assistant, Valerie Griffith, you two are the best; thank you doesn't begin to say it all. To my editor, Carole DeSanti, girlfriend, your words of wisdom are always right on time. To the staff at Dutton, thank you all for the time and effort you've invested in my work. To all my homegirls in Ohio, Alaska, Atlanta, and New York, I love you all. To my Seattle sister circle,

Charlotte Watson Sherman, Carletta Wilson, Colleen McElroy, Alma Arnold, Marilyn Fullen Collins, Faith Davis, Jody Kim, Doris Harris, Barbara Thomas, Gail Myers, Ester and Zola Muford, Marsha Leslie, Amy Lely, Pat Dawson, Chyla Axtell, and Kim Holland, thank you, thank you, thank you for all of your supportive love. I would also like to extend a special thank you to Brenda Freeman, Marie Iman, and Rachel Warwick for making me laugh and keeping me on my toes. To my clinical colleagues and support staff at G.H.C. Central Mental Health, your patience and heartfelt support have meant so much to me, thanks, you've been wonderful. To my son Michael, my adopted son Raymond, and of course Boggie, I love you guys with all my heart.

Introduction

"Be careful what you pray for . . ."   —Mama

Girlfriend to Girlfriend is a short collection of sage wisdom, witty responses, and heartfelt comments I've heard from sisters individually and collectively in sister circles across the nation in the past several months. In my many contacts with Black women across the nation, I've recognized that as sisters we've dealt with the trials and pitfalls of life, and while many of our lives may go in different directions, we've often traveled similar paths in managing to find a variety of ways to cope. I've discovered that as sisters we're some powerful teachers and the lessons we've learned in our lives deserve to be passed on. As I listened to the sisters in different cities and states I recognized four major themes: Self-Care; Family, Friends, and Lovers; Health Issues; and Daily

Struggles. I collected a sampling of quotes representing these four themes and broke them down into sections that speak to these issues. In the first section of this book, "Defining Ourselves," I included quotes that address the issues of self-care; "Family, Friends, and Lovers," Section Two, focuses on coping with intimate others; "In Sickness and Health" deals with concerns of a physical nature; and "Over the Back Fence" deals with our daily struggles in life. In sharing the everyday wisdom of the sisters on these pages, I found that their words closely echoed my own thoughts and feelings at different times in my life. Let's face it—sometimes it's reassuring to recognize and to know that we are truly not alone in how we view our world, and somewhere sisters just like us have found ways to support their lives and maintain a sense of courage. Following the quotes I've taken the liberty of adding a few words of my own—sometimes something just needs to be said. I've also added affirmations to the sisters' words, 'cause like I said before, we're some powerful teachers and what good is a lesson if we can't apply the learning to our own life in some way. You'll find, as I did, that these sisters'

words are sassy, brassy, and full of spunk, but at the same time their words share a supportive wisdom by offering hope, empowerment, prayers, and homegirl encouragement to get you through the minute-to-minute obstacle course called daily living. These quotations are from us, for us, and about us. All the quotations, just like the sisters who speak the words, invite you to look into a mirror and love yourself just a tad bit more today than you did yesterday. If you can't find a quotation to fit your mood, attitude, or situation, take out your pen and create one. We've left some empty pages at the back of the book so you can always have the last word. So from one girlfriend to another, this book is your personal invitation to join the sister circle.

I

Defining Ourselves

"... If we do not define ourselves for ourselves, we will be defined by others—for their use and to our detriment."

—Audre Lorde

"**H**oney, it's a jungle out there and I just found out I ain't the queen."

"I hear you, girlfriend, but ain't it nice to know that you don't have to be in charge of that mess."

I overheard this snippet of conversation between two sisters as we were standing in line at the local bank. Now maybe it's my nature, or just good training, but I often hear little jewels of wisdom for myself in other folks' everyday conversations. One of my favorites came from a sister-friend of mine. When I complained to her about how the job and everything else in my life was getting me down, she pulled my coat and told me, "Girlfriend, what you need is an I-L-L day, which stands for *I Love Life*, and I pamper myself like you wouldn't believe." Needless to say, this sister-

friend didn't need to say another word 'cause I got the message loud and clear, and I've taken the liberty of inserting an I-L-L day into my monthly schedule.

Just as these sisters have pointed out the value of defining how we view and take care of ourselves, so will the sisters in this section help you pay closer attention to your self-care—and encourage you to make the kinds of choices that help us become who we need to be.

 Self-Acceptance

You know this morning I got up early enough to sit on the back porch with a cup of coffee and watch the sunrise. Without even think'n about it I found myself kick'n it with the Creator, being thankful for my life and all that's in my life right now. Sometimes with all the mess that's go'n on around me I forget that I'm truly a lovable and worthwhile sister.

—Libby

With all the hustle and bustle it's so easy to forget just how important we are in the daily scheme of things. We take care of this, fix that, and comfort those we love, rarely taking a moment for ourselves. Take a second—no, take a whole minute right now and give thanks for being just who you are, a beautiful Black woman with the courage to carry on with the many demands in your life.

I'M A LOVABLE AND WORTHWHILE
BLACK WOMAN EVERY DAY

 # Being Flexible

I wish I had more time to spend on myself, but shoot, between go'n to work, tak'n care of kids, and look'n after the house, where am I supposed to find any kind of free time?

—Janie

It's not that we don't have time, it's just that we get so locked into our daily routine until it's hard to imagine doing things differently. My mother used to say with a great deal of pride a few years ago, "Honey, my house is so clean till you can eat off the floors." Momi had a heart attack three years ago, and while she continues to keep a clean, neat house, she's become more fond of her health than her floors. We've got to start being more flexible with our time demands to reduce our stress.

I'M WILLING TO BE FLEXIBLE

☕ Trying to Do It All

Honey, the only thing I have in common with Superwoman is gender.

—Zoey

I'm convinced that if we could meet all the daily demands heaped on our female shoulders we would make Superwoman look like a slug. We don't possess unlimited magic powers, we possess human ability which does have limits. Not being able to do it all isn't a sign of weakness, it's a reminder that we're human.

I'M ONLY HUMAN

 # Self-Care

Come hell or high water every second and fourth Saturday of the month belongs to me. I go and get my hair and nails done and if my girlfriends can get away we have lunch. If they can't make it I take myself to a movie. I learned a long time ago that do'n a little something for myself made me feel better about do'n for everybody else.

—Margie

Today's lesson in self-care is, I will do kind things for myself, I will do kind things for myself, I will do kind things for myself. Repeat this sentence ten times each hour, for twelve hours each day for the rest of your life.

I WILL MAKE MY SELF-CARE
A PRIORITY

Humor

Remember to Laugh —Julia's To-Do List

Right after my divorce things were so hectic in my life that I would have to make myself little notes and lists just to keep up. I was thumbing through an old notebook the other night and found this notation at the top of one of my lists. Things still get pretty hectic in my life and I still make lists, but I don't need to remind myself to laugh anymore, it's automatic now. As you will find from reading this book, I tend to look for the humor in most situations because I've discovered that laughter has the ability to heal even the most damaged heart. I can be intensely serious too, when it's needed, but humor will always be important in my life.

REMEMBER TO LAUGH

 # Appearances

Keep your body clean, your hair combed, and your clothes neat. The good Lord don't love ugly and he ain't crazy 'bout pretty neither but he'll love ya and you'll love yourself if ya always remember to be clean.

—Annie

With all the hype about looks these days, I have to work at remembering Mama's words, which were generally spoken when as a child I begged for something that I thought might enhance my status in the world of my peers.

I AM BEAUTIFUL JUST AS I AM

 Self-Love

There used to be a time when I looked in the mirror and hated what I saw: I was overweight, my teeth were crooked, and my hair was so thin until you could see my scalp. I didn't have a real reason for not looking after myself, except that I just hadn't made these things a priority. Last year I made the decision to start taking care of me. I started putting aside money from every paycheck and joined a gym; I asked my doctor to help me with a diet and I attend O.A. (Overeaters Anonymous) meetings once a week, and I got my hair weaved. By Christmas I'll have enough saved to pay the deductible for my braces. People say you should love yourself for what's inside, but I couldn't get past how I looked on the outside in order to appreciate myself as a whole person. At least now I like enough of what I see that I can start loving me.

—Tami

Everyone has their own definition of self-love: My definition is self-honesty. If making physical changes in your appearance helps you to love yourself, then make the changes. There's a lot of hype and arm-chair speculation about Black entertainers who make changes in their personal appearance, but I've never

heard any of these entertainers say that they didn't love themselves. If changing something about yourself helps you to love who you are on the inside, then by all means *do it*.

I LOVE MYSELF

 # Self-Reward

Hey, girlfriend, I caught this great sale at Kmart yesterday. I'm talk'n major blue-light special. Well honey, I got the kids a few things and just for the hell of it I got me not one but two pair of shoes. While I was in the check-out line I started to feel a little guilty, I didn't really need those shoes, but I liked them. The longer I stood there the more I started think'n, I work hard every day and I do right by my kids, and spend'n a little piece of change on myself ain't gonna break the bank. I swear, sometimes I really have to work at remembering I deserve the right to reward myself every once in a while.

—Vergie

Sometimes we need to give ourselves reminders that we're doing a good job with our lives.

I DESERVE THE RIGHT TO
REWARD MYSELF

 *Self-Definition*

Whenever we would get into an argument my ex-boyfriend accused me of not act'n Black. He was try'n to hurt me and at first it worked, 'cause he had the power to cut deep. Then I figured out, Hey! he ain't all that, and if I wasn't Black enough for him then he could just keep on step'n. I know who I am.

—Cindy

Whenever we place too much value on someone else's opinion of who we are we give up the power to truly choose how to define ourselves in this world. Remember, girlfriend, our Blackness is not defined by what we do or don't do, it's our birthright.

I HAVE THE POWER TO
DEFINE MYSELF

 # Strength

I found that other people telling me I was a strong Black woman was just their way of leaning on me.

—Carrie

We're not strong Black women, we're Black women who have learned through the years how to endure pain, suffering, and loss. These things didn't make us strong, they made us exceptionally tolerant Black women. As Black women we've got to start encouraging others to define us in ways that allow our humanness as women to shine through.

I'M MORE THAN A STRONG
BLACK WOMAN

 Selflessness

Wanda Jean got evicted again, so her and the kids are go'n be moving in again. I was go'n retire in June, but with three extra mouths to feed I guess that's out the question. Lord I ain't never gonna get no rest, seems like every time Fred and me plan on do'n a little somethin' for ourselves one of the kids need somethin'.

—Velma

"My job is to do for you all, I get my rewards later on" (meaning in heaven). This was Mama's response whenever we encouraged her to take a much-needed break. Now when I was young Mama's words didn't faze me much, maybe it was because "later on" didn't hold much meaning. But as I grew older I came to understand that "later on" meant that Mama would have to die before she claimed her rewards, and I had to seriously reevaluate this concept. When we deprive ourselves at the expense of doing for others, the only rewards we get are to be worn out and tired. When we do for others, let it be from a sense of free will and not duty.

I DON'T HAVE TO RESCUE OTHERS

 # Self-Criticism

My kids are always accusing me of being hard on them, and they're right. I'm hard on them 'cause I want the best for them. Shoot! It's like I told them, I'm hard on them and I'm hard on myself, ain't nothing easy in life.

—Vy

Life isn't easy and it isn't hard, it's just life: no more and no less. When we view the world as a cold, hard, lonely place and we're living in that world, what are we saying about ourselves? Someone once told me that self-criticism was a first cousin to everlasting shame. No one deserves to feel ashamed of their life.

I CAN BE GENTLE WITH MYSELF

 *Determination*

I had to feed my kids, so I just told myself, I can do this. I just believed in me.

—Lestine

I'm a Taurus so I've heard all the jokes about being bull-headed and stubborn. But you know what? I don't mind, because those traits speak to my determination of character. My personal motto is: If there's a way, I'll find it, and if there isn't a way, I'll make one. What's your personal motto?

I WILL ALWAYS BELIEVE IN ME

 Self-Encouragement

I just told myself that I could handle the situation. I didn't really have a plan or nothing, but I just kept telling myself in my head, "I can do this, I can do this," and before I knew it I was handling it.

—Lestine

I talk to myself. It's no big deal, really! In the privacy of our minds we all talk to ourselves. I can just imagine you saying to yourselves right now, "This girlfriend has really gone off the deep end 'cause I know I don't be talking to myself." Well, let me reassure you right now by saying that everybody talks to themselves. Check it out! How many times in the past week have you thought, "I need to do ..." or "I should do ..." Bingo! Those thoughts are you talking to yourself. Our minds are the most powerful part of our bodies, and when we give our minds powerful messages such as "I can do this," we can choose to respond to that message. The problem is that we don't often listen to the messages that we give ourselves. Now would be a good time to start paying attention to that personal self-talk. Tell yourself how good you are, and how productive you've been today. Now listen to your words of encouragement.

I CAN ENCOURAGE MYSELF

 # Potential

I used to get so tickled when my granddaddy would look at me when I was little and say to my grandmama, "Yes sir, Goldie, that lil' girl right there got some potential." I didn't know what potential meant back then but it sure made me feel good to hear him say it. I wish granddaddy had lived to see me graduate from law school, 'cause his belief in my potential helped me to believe in myself.

—Jo

I'm a big believer in the idea that every one of us possesses some form of unique talent that makes us special. Some of us have received encouragement to explore our special talent, and some of us are still waiting to hear just how special we are in this world. Let me say right now, I'm a believer in you because I know you're a woman of potential.

I AM A WOMAN WITH POTENTIAL

 # Dreams

I had such big dreams for myself once, and I just don't know what happened.

—Tess

Outside of hurting someone, there is only one other major sin: not pursuing your dreams. My mother used to say, If wishes were dreams beggars would fly. Maybe beggars would rather wish than work toward their dreams, but it doesn't have to be that way. If you have time to wish, then you have time to put energy into pursuing your dream. Dreams don't just happen—we do things to make them happen. So put your energy where it counts, into making your dreams come true.

I'M WILLING TO MAKE MY DREAMS COME TRUE

 # Questions

Everybody always laughs at me 'cause I ask questions all the time. Even when I was little I used to always ask questions, I can't help it.

—LaShawn

Asking questions is very healthy; it's one of the ways that we acquire knowledge for ourselves.

QUESTIONS PROVIDE ME
WITH KNOWLEDGE

 # Choices

I learned a long time ago that not everybody was go'n agree with some of the things that I did in my life. But it's like this: I'm grown and I don't feel like I got to explain myself to anybody.

—Cassie

As a child I learned the value of having and making choices early in life. Momi would allow me to pick out what I wanted to wear to church or school. If my clothing selection met with her standards of being neat, clean, and a proper fit I was allowed to wear it; if not, I was sent back to make another selection. As an adult my choices haven't always been as simple, nor do I have my mother's approval or disapproval to guide me. I've come to understand that along with adult choices come adult responsibilities. I won't always receive guidance or approval for the choices I'll make in my lifetime, but my right to make a choice is worth the responsibility I'm willing to take as an adult.

AS AN ADULT I CAN MAKE MY OWN
CHOICES IN LIFE

 # Taking Risks

Folks thought I was crazy when I quit the post office to go back to school.

—Irene

Sometimes to get what we really want we have to take risks. Mama always told me that nothing beats a failure but a try, and at eighty plus years Mama has a lot of wisdom under her belt. If we're not willing to take a risk, what are we willing to do?

I CAN TAKE RISKS IN MY LIFE

☕ *Opportunity*

My *supervisor offered me the chance to open and manage a new store in Princeton, New Jersey, next fall. I don't know though, at first I was really excited, now I just don't know. I'd have to move and get the kids settled in school and all. Plus I don't know anybody there, it's so far away from my family. I'll probably take it, but it's kind of scary . . . you know what I mean.*

—Kendel

Opportunity is such a tease—you're hungry and here's this carrot dangling in front of your nose. Now you want to eat, but you're not really sure you want a carrot, you could wait and maybe something else tasty will come along but then again you can't be sure about that either. What to do? What to do? I don't have an answer but I do know that you can fix carrots in a number of tasty ways.

I CAN TAKE ADVANTAGE OF MY OPPORTUNITIES

 Sexual Preference

Oh, I get it, you're one of those liberal Blacks, you like everybody.

—Kathy

This statement was directed at me during a discussion group. We were talking about sexuality and one of the sisters made a derogatory remark about lesbians and gays, and I called her on it. I would like to share with you the response I gave: "I've never thought of myself as liberal, but I'm not into labels much; however, I do make a habit of standing up and speaking out about what I believe in. I didn't choose to be Black or to be born female, however I'm quite proud and happy to be both. I don't believe that people choose their sexual preference and they have every right to be proud and enjoy their sexuality. You all may not think it's the same type of thing, but from where I stand and what I see discrimination and oppression feels and looks just as ugly. As far as liking everybody, I have a firm and what I think is a very healthy dislike of anyone who uses fear and violence as a means to control others. Let's move on."

MY SEXUAL PREFERENCE IS A NATURAL PART OF WHO I AM

 # Respect

There's only one thing that a stranger can give me that I'll take without question—respect.

—Mavis

When we carry ourselves with dignity the only outcome we can expect is the right to respect.

I DESERVE RESPECT

 Creativity

I wish I could write. —Toni

Do it, do it, do it. Write, paint, draw, sing, play an instrument, take pictures, do whatever you need to do to express your creative urges. You don't need to be good at fulfilling your creative desire, you just have to fill the need. Fill your creative need for yourself. This is yours; it doesn't need to be, dare I say it, "perfect," it just has to be yours. Talent isn't what this is about, having fun is, so please don't wish, just *do*, be creative.

CREATIVITY IS A PART OF MY LIFE

 # Goals

I signed the papers for my house yesterday. It took me three years but I did it.

—Angie

Goals are wonderful blueprints for action. When we set goals we're giving ourselves a message that we're planning to make a change in our lives. Being able to set daily, monthly, and yearly goals allows us to look forward to taking action in our lives. Start today, start small, but start setting goals.

I CAN SET GOALS FOR MYSELF

 *Travel*

One of these days I'm go'n travel.   —Wanda

We let too many days pass with wishes on our lips. To travel is to enjoy one of life's greatest pleasures. If this sounds like a commercial you can skip this page, but I've heard so many sisters say they've wanted to travel so I want to encourage every one of them to do it. It doesn't have to be a big major trip or cost thousands of dollars, and even if it does your pleasure is worth every penny. Buy a bus or train ticket and ride across the state or the country and just sightsee. I guess I love travel so much because the memories are everlasting. I can lose my money, a thief could steal all my shoes, and I may misplace my books, but I'll always have my memories of Paris. So tell me, where did you say you were going?

I WILL PLAN TO TRAVEL

 # Pride

Honey, if pride goes before a fall then let me fall all over myself, 'cause I sure do feel proud of myself this evenin'.

—Lettie

As soon as I get my magical powers I'm going to wave my special wand and sprinkle proud dust on every child, woman, and man in the universe. We all deserve to feel proud of ourselves at least twice a day, when we get up in the morning and when we lay our head on the pillow at night. We don't need special awards or occasions in order to feel proud of ourselves, we just need to say, "I'm proud of who I am."

I CAN FEEL PROUD OF MYSELF

II

Family, Friends, and Lovers

Family, friends, and lovers: Most of us have at least one if not all three present in our lives on a daily basis. The roles we play in raising our families, supporting our friends, and sharing intimacies with our lovers nurture our sense of self. However, it's sometimes hard to recognize our own needs when we're meeting the needs of others day in and day out. The sisters in this section have started paying attention to what's missing for them, and there might be a chance that you'll hear your voice too.

 Family Support

I love my family, but Lord they sure do make me tired. Daddy's heart ain't good. Mama's git'n on in years and just can't take the load like she used to. My oldest sister's got four mouths to feed by herself. Junior's out there act'n the fool, strung out on that mess, and Baby Sis, well she's doing better but she's got a big-time alcohol problem. I haven't even told them my plans to leave Jimmy, 'cause it would just lead to more confusion than it's worth. I know they would be there for me if they could, but mostly everybody's sit'n around wait'n on the other shoe to drop. I'm so tired of wait'n on that shoe to fall, 'til sometimes I just want to knock it off.

—Tess

It would be nice if our family could be there for us in our time of need, but let's face facts, sometimes it's just not possible. Look at the ways in which your family can and has offered support in the past, and then allow yourself to move on. Look to gain the support you need in the present from others whom you feel close to and respect.

I CAN RECEIVE SUPPORT OUTSIDE OF
MY FAMILY

 *Support*

Sometimes I have to remind myself that a closed mouth don't get fed.

—Lucy

I'll often hear sisters complain that family members or friends aren't supportive. When I ask if they've asked for support, very often the answer is no. Sometimes I'll get answers like "If they cared (or loved me) they'd know," and my next question of "How" is met with dead silence. If we want the support of others we have to be willing to ask for it. True, asking will make us vulnerable, but at least we've done our part. I've discovered others are often willing to be supportive when they're given a chance.

I CAN ASK FOR WHAT I NEED

 # *Privacy*

There are days when I just want to run away from home and never come back. "Mama where's this . . . Honey have you seen my . . . Velma can you do. . . . The only time I can get any peace is when I'm in the bathroom and even then, when they know I'm in there, they knock on the door.

—Velma

We have a right to privacy, in fact we need it in order to collect our thoughts and restore our sense of emotional balance. Select a time each day or evening that will belong just to you. It doesn't need to be a lot of time, but make it your personal time. Let your family know in advance that you're going to be taking this time and that you won't be available except in extreme emergencies. You can decide what types of emergencies you'll respond to.

I HAVE A RIGHT TO
SOME PRIVATE TIME

 # Anger

Girl, the other night I caught Tanya sneak'n out the house try'n to go to some party after I told her no way. Honey, I was fit to be tied and it was all I could do to keep myself from get'n the belt and wear'n her lil' skinny butt out. But I was determined not to let my anger get the best of me, so I just told Miss Tanya that she would have the pleasure of my company for the next two weekends.

—Tess

We all have a boiling point, and if we're human, which we are, there's going to be a time when we let go and just blow. Many of us are afraid of our anger, but actually anger is a very healthy emotion. It's what we do with our anger that generally leads us into trouble like hurting ourselves or each other. When anger turns to rage and violence it moves from being constructive and healthy to destructive and unhealthy. Here are some healthy ways of handling anger: Take a walk or run, go to the gym and work it out physically, lock yourself in a room and yell at the top of your lungs, write a nasty letter and burn it. These are just a few suggestions and

they may not be right for you, but whatever you do, don't let your anger become destructive.

MY ANGER DOESN'T HAVE TO BE
A DESTRUCTIVE ACT

🍵 Responsibility

You know sometimes I believe that folks think I'm queen of the universe. Every time something happens, here they all come look'n to me to take care of it. I used to like it, 'cause I felt like they looked up to me, but now that I got a life it just seems like don't nobody want to take responsibility. After Daddy passed, I took care of making all the arrangements and everything and I didn't ask not one soul to lift a finger. Now the house has got to be sold, and the realtor told me it needs some work. I got a new job and my own family to care for, so I asked my sister and brothers to take care of getting that done. Well, the realtor called yesterday to ask when the work was go'n to get started so he could list the house. It turns out nobody's done a damn thing.

—Nettie

Being responsible is tricky business. When we're too responsible others tend to depend on us too much. At the same time, we may end up feeling used because others aren't responsible enough. Sometimes it helps to put limits on what we're willing to be responsible for, and stick to it. If others don't follow through on their duties, then it's on them.

I CAN ONLY BE RESPONSIBLE FOR
WHAT I CAN DO

 *Advice*

Marlon ran away from home again last week. I know he's uptown staying with one of his school friends, but I'm sick of this mess. I got a good mind to call his father and tell him to come get his butt for good. But then he wouldn't be able to get to school and I know his father won't make him go. My friend Joyce says I should just put him out and let him fend for hisself, my mother told me she'd give me the money to send him down South to my brother. I don't know which way to turn, and everybody means well but all their advice is just confusing me more.

—Karen

Have you ever noticed how many people have solutions to your problems? It doesn't matter that these same solutions didn't work for the person offering them. Shoot, half the time that person doesn't even have the same problem. My friend Zoey says that if advice was any good it wouldn't be so free, and I'm inclined to agree. Most of the time we just need the space to talk out a problem, and given the time we'll work out our own solution. No one has a better solution for your problem than you.

I CAN LISTEN TO MY OWN ADVICE

Shame and Guilt

My son was part of a gang drive-by shooting last year and was sent to prison. I don't know, I thought I was a good parent. I mean, I didn't raise him to be like that, I tried to give him and the rest of the kids what they needed. But I had to work and I couldn't be everywhere at once. I don't know, I just don't know anymore.

—Pat

I've always thought of shame and guilt as hostage keepers. They invade our mind and soul without warning, leaving our thoughts bound in doubt and our bodies racked in fear. The more we struggle against the intense bindings of shame and guilt the more helpless we feel. There's only one escape—reasoning. That's right, reasoning. Shame and guilt can't stand up to solid reasoning because it wears them out. Shame and guilt are thoughts that are generally connected to the past in some way. We think about what we "should have," "could have," or "would have" done differently, but there's no way to recapture the past so when we have those thoughts in the present we get caught in the tangled web of shame and guilt, which is more harmful than helpful. If you did something that makes you feel bad in the past can you do something now in the present to

help make up for it? I also want to say here that we are not responsible for what others have done to us, including acts of sexual or physical abuse. That shame and guilt belongs to that person, not you. If you find that you continually have problems wrestling your shame and guilt to the floor, please talk to a therapist.

I CAN LET GO OF MY SHAME
AND GUILT

 # Welfare

My family's ashamed of me 'cause I had to apply for state aid. It's not like I want to make a habit of it, but it ain't like I'm sitting at home doing nothing. I'm taking parenting classes and when the baby gets older my case worker said I could apply for college courses.

—Tangie

I've always wondered how it is that we never hear about the welfare success stories. After all, with thousands of people on welfare there must be someone somewhere who did the program and managed to succeed. I also wondered if the only people on welfare are Black and female. I asked a journalist friend of mine these questions and the answers I received were as follows: Plenty of people succeed on welfare, it allows them to go back to school, train for jobs, and get a start that might not otherwise be possible. But the thing is, those who make it don't make good copy (stories). Not everybody on welfare is Black and female, in fact several years ago government statistics showed that the largest percentage of welfare recipients lived in the midwestern region of the United States (farm country). However, most of the media focused on the inner-city population. I thought this information was interesting but not sur-

prising. Let's face it, Black folks in trouble always seems to make good copy, but for whom? Welfare is a resource—nothing less, nothing more. If you need it, use it. There's nothing shameful about using resources when you need them.

I AM ABLE TO USE AVAILABLE
RESOURCES WISELY

Family Dysfunction

Girlfriend, it's like this, I'm not interested in what the experts say about folks who come from so-called dysfunctional families. My family may wear that sorry label, but I ain't hav'n none of it. My frame of mind tells me that labels are for canned goods and I ain't got time to sit on nobody's shelf. When folks look at me they see me, not my family. I'm as normal as I want to be.

—Cassie

Just as all families have functional characteristics, they also have dysfunctional characteristics. As a family member you too will have functional and dysfunctional characteristics. The good news is as an adult and as an individual you can choose the family characteristics that you want in your life.

I AM MY OWN INDIVIDUAL

 Role Models

I wasn't always around for my kids when they was growing up, I was serving time for drugs. So I had to give my kids over to my mother to raise. She did good by them, making them go to school and church and stuff. I been out of prison for three years now, and I can't be a mom to my kids 'cause they all grown with kids of they own, but I can be a friend and a grandmother for my grandkids. I'm clean and I'm in counseling so I'm learning things that I want to pass on to the kids.

—Willie

I believe in angels, not the rosy-cheeked, floating-white-dress-celestial type of angel that only folks embraced by a certain kind of light can see. I believe in the everyday kind of angel, like sis Willie. She's lived a life, made some mistakes, and is working on passing on the lessons she's learned. Sistah Willie is a role model and that's all angels are—models of what life looks like in our everyday lives. Being a role model isn't about being perfect, it's about passing on life lessons. We're all role models in our own unique ways. I guess you could say we're all angels, for ourselves, for each other, and for our little sisters.

I'M A ROLE MODEL FOR MY SISTERS

Parenting Rules

I ain't go'n lie, I love my kids like the air I breathe. But I'll tell you just like I told them, God didn't put me on this earth to take grief from nobody including my own. So if you're go'n be in my house and you don't want me in your business, then you best keep your business together, 'cause the first time your trouble knocks on my front door, that front door is go'n hit you in the behind.

—Flo

My definition of parenthood is sainthood, 'cause this is without a doubt the toughest responsibility or test of sanity on God's green earth. But you know, I wouldn't trade it for the world. As adults, remember, it's our job to make the rules, and it's our kids' unoffical job to test the rules, and believe me, they will test every rule ever made. Please remember to start your list of rules with two things in mind, love and safety, because these are the two that count the most.

IT'S MY RESPONSIBILITY AS A PARENT TO MAKE THE RULES

 # *Parenting*

Well, the way I see it, kids and groceries have at least one thing in common—expiration dates. When groceries reach their expiration date and start spoiling we can throw them away. But when kids reach their childhood expiration date, they become adults and start having memories. We've got to start think'n about what type of childhood memories we want our kids to have as adults.

—Zoey

Have you hugged your child today? When's the last time you did something special with your child? These are the types of things that encourage happy memories.

I CAN GIVE MY CHILDREN
LOVING MEMORIES

 Expectations

I don't expect my kids to do any more around the house than I would do.

—Tess

I used to hate hearing this statement for two reasons when I was a kid: Number one, it generally meant that something around the house needed to be done or redone as the case often was, and number two, both of my parents were major work maniacs with standards that made Mount Rainier look like a molehill. Personally I don't blame my parents for having high expectations, it's just that I've always had a hard time keeping up. As an adult I have to work at keeping my expectations for myself and others in line with personal capabilities. It's fine to have high expectations, just don't make them too high to reach.

I WILL KEEP MY EXPECTATIONS
IN LINE

 Compassion

Every year on Thanksgiving I take my kids down to the mission to serve dinner to the homeless. I want them to know just what they got to be thankful for.

—Brenda

"I thought I was abused because I had no shoes, until I met a man who had no feet."

—J. M. Braude

Whenever I'm in the mood for an old-fashioned pity party, I just remember the Braude quote. Then I get off my butt and go do something for somebody else—volunteer at a shelter, donate food and clothing to homeless agencies, make telephone calls for health-based charities, visit sick friends. There's always something we can do for somebody else, we just have to be willing to lend a helping hand.

I CAN ALWAYS LEND
A HELPING HAND

 # Family Reunion

Me and the kids are go'n home in August for the yearly family reunion. Sometimes think'n about get'n together with everybody and all the fun we'll be hav'n for a few weeks in the summer is the only thing that keeps me go'n during the year.

—Yolanda

When I was younger and living at home I couldn't wait to be on my own. Now as an adult, I can't wait for the special times when we have our family gatherings: Momi, Daddy, all of my sisters and brothers, in-laws, nieces, and nephews gathering at each other's homes, cooking up a storm, playing cards, telling stories, and laughing like there's no tomorrow. I treasure these family times, and while we have our problems, we all know that we can count on each other for comfort and support. When I'm around my family I'm often reminded of Dorothy in the *Wizard of Oz*, when she says, "There's no place like home, there's no place like home." I agree with Dorothy, there's no place like home, and when I'm with my family, I'm truly home.

MY FAMILY IS ONE SOURCE OF
MY STRENGTH

 # Celebration

I told my kids that this year we're go'n start celebrating Kwanzaa 'cause I want them to start knowing more 'bout their African-American heritage.

—Josie

There are so few times when we get the opportunity to collectively celebrate who we are culturally and ethnically. Kwanzaa is the perfect time for all of us to come together and renew our spirit and rejoice in our heritage.

I CAN CELEBRATE WHO I AM

 *Sharing*

My family and good friends all know that if I got a dime, they got a nickel, 'cause that's just the way I am.

—Carrie

Growing up with eight sisters and brothers, it was tough to be selfish. We shared everything from food to beds, and honey if I had a dime for every time I uttered the phrase, "When I git grown I'm have my own. . . ." Well, so much for being grown, I'm still sharing just about everything I own, but I do draw the line at underwear. I think it's kind of hard to live in this world and not share something of ourselves, and I'm not just speaking of material things here. We share our time, energy, and knowledge with others all the time, but these aren't the only things we share: We share a smile, a hello, a glance, and thoughts all the time. Think of the many ways in which you share every day. Maybe you'll even want to expand your list a little.

I'M WILLING TO SHARE WITH OTHERS

🍵 Community

I've lived in the Rainier Valley for forty-five years, twenty of them years I been in the same house. I know everybody on my block, and I'm proud of the fact that they know me.

—Lena

I miss the old neighborhoods where everybody knew everybody else. We had our own system of neighborhood watch during those days, because if Miss Gracie down the street saw something or someone who didn't belong on our street, she was going to find out what was going on and spread the word. I can remember thinking Miss Gracie was a nosy old lady, but I never had to worry about my safety when I was out playing, because if Momi wasn't around to watch us, Miss Gracie was right there watching our every move.

I don't know or remember when we stopped looking out for each other, and our families, but I'm all for bringing that sense of community back into style. I'm willing to be a nosy neighbor if it means our children can feel and be protected or that our property is safe. A sense of community is a sense of feeling cared about.

MY COMMUNITY IS IMPORTANT TO ME

 Unity

It seems to me that we work overtime finding fault. Sisters dis'n each other and brothers too, there's always something wrong or somebody to blame for what ain't right. I ain't say'n that we all gotta be best friends or nothing, but it would be nice to show each other a little respect now and then.

—Marie

Mama always told me that misery loved company, and you know I believe she's right. I wonder what would happen if we all made the decision not to say anything disrespectful about one another for just one day. Remember, it's always the little things that divide us.

I AM ONE WITH MY SISTERS
AND BROTHERS

 *Disagreement*

It's like this, girlfriend, my mouth ain't no Bible, and if the truth be told I been known to overstate the truth a time or two. But I'm open to folks disagreeing with me, just as long as they grant me the same courtesy.

—Vy

I don't celebrate very many religious holidays, but Lent is my all-time favorite. Lent is a time of atonement, ridding myself of old baggage, and Lent is also a time of renewal, of opening my emotional and spiritual doors to create room for personal growth. Several years ago I created emotional and spiritual space for others to openly disagree with my personal view of the world. This was a major step for me, because it meant that I had to be willing to give up the need to be perceived by others in a certain way. I can now allow others to have and share their view of the world without trying to convince them that they need to think or believe as I do. I can still have my point of view without begrudging those who have a different viewpoint.

I CAN AGREE TO DISAGREE

 # Sisterhood

When I think of sisterhood I think about my sorority sisters—I mean, this is a powerful group of Black sisters. As a group we do things for the community, and some of us are really tight friends. But what I love the most is the fellowship and the fact that we all have a sense of purpose and mission.

—Grace

We don't all belong to sororities, but as Black women we can share a sense of sisterhood. When you see a sister on the street or in a store, offer a friendly greeting. Participate in activities in your community that reach out to young sisters and brothers too. Join your local chapter of the National Black Women's Health Project and help promote healthy lifestyles for Black women, or join or start a sister circle or sister support group. We gather strength in our togetherness.

I FIND MY STRENGTH IN SISTERHOOD

 Commitment

Me and Tommy been together fourteen years, and we've had our ups and downs, but the bottom line is when it's all been said and done we're there for each other through thick and thin.

—Shawna

Momi takes great pride in saying, "I've been with your daddy longer then I was with my mother." My parents have been married fifty-three years, and I can testify to the fact that it ain't been easy. I have a lot of love and a great deal of respect for my parents and their commitment to each other. As a woman who's tried the union and commitment of marriage, I've discovered the complexity of shared togetherness requires not only love but a willingness to create a joint spirit.

MY COMMITMENT IS A MUTUAL AGREEMENT

☕ Partnership

*Honey, this is the nineties—I don't just want a rela-
tionship, I want a partnership, 'cause being together is
more than just being in love. I want to be with someone
who can give what I give—respect, trust, and love. No,
sir, I don't need no half step'n in the name of love.*

—Cheryl

Choosing to be in an intimate relationship can be
a very exciting and scary process. You're learning
how to be part of a couple, while still in the process
of being an individual. I think it takes three things
to be in a good partnership: (1) respect for each
other, (2) shared expectations, and (3) the willingness to be flexible. The love you share with each
other will help you openly communicate about these
three items.

I'M WORTHY OF A TRUE PARTNERSHIP
IN LIFE

Dependency

I think the major thing I did wrong in my relationship was depending on my partner too much. I wanted him to be there for me the way I was for him, and he just couldn't handle it. Maybe I'm wrong but I thought that's what love was all about.

—Donna

We all have different needs in relationships, and that's fine. However, it becomes a problem when we forget to talk to each other about our specific needs. Dependency needs are tricky because we often don't recognize that we want or need until after the fact. Saying to someone that you're depending on them to pick you up every day after work is very different from saying, "I'm depending on you to help me get through this crisis." It's okay to depend on others, but it helps if they know what you're depending on them to do.

I HAVE TO LET OTHERS KNOW
I'M DEPENDING ON THEM TO FILL
SPECIFIC NEEDS

 # Relationship Abuse

Honey, if it hurts I'm history, 'cause love ain't sup-posed to hurt.

—Zoey

When I was much younger I believed that the only way you could really prove how much you loved someone was by taking whatever your partner did to you in stride. I'm not that young anymore and neither is my definition of love. I now know and understand that healthy loving relationships are not born out of nor thrive on abusive pain of any kind. Just in case you're not clear on what I mean by abusive pain, here's my definition: any type of physical, emotional, psychological, verbal, or sexual encounter that frightens or hurts you. I totally agree with my friend Zoey on this one—love ain't supposed to hurt.

LOVE IS NEVER PAINFUL

Breakup of Relationships

Girlfriend, when me and Harmon broke up you would have thought somebody died, by the way I carried on. Honey, I was a full-blown mess, stopped eat'n, crying all the time, and no talk'n to nobody for days. After 'bout a week I snapped out of it, and I just kept tell'n myself, I was a good woman before him, I was a good woman with him, and I can be a good woman without him. Don't get me wrong, it'll be three months on the fifteenth and I'm still a little tender around the edges, but I know I'll be alright.

—Bettie

I've heard rumors that women who are in relationships are happier than single women. Thank goodness this is only a rumor, because I'm willing to put myself out on a limb by saying there is no proof to back up this claim. While it's true that some women feel happier and more content in a relationship, there are just as many women—and men, for that matter—equally happy and content being single. When we break up with someone we don't forfeit our right to happiness, and while we may be emotional or upset at the time of the split, if we're willing to

give ourselves time to heal, we will and can move on with our lives. And who knows, we may even find some happiness in being single.

I'LL ALWAYS BE A GOOD WOMAN
WITH OR WITHOUT A PARTNER

 # Being Alone

I thought life was over when Chester left, and the kids got grown and moved away. Now it's like being alone ain't so bad. I enjoy not having to worry about nobody but myself, I cook when I want, visit friends, and putter in the yard. I ain't say'n that it wouldn't be nice to have someone around every now and then, but for the most part I can handle bein' by myself.

—Josie

"Momi, I don't have nobody to play with."

"Play by yourself, you weren't born with no twin."

Momi, bless her heart, taught me very early that being alone didn't mean that I had to be lonely. This is not a lesson that many of us were fortunate enough to get as children. When we take the time to be alone we can make space to discover our hidden treasures. I use my alone time to write poetry (true, it's bad poetry most of the time, but it's mine), I go for walks, I talk with my God, and sometimes I just count the number of red cars that come down my street. Take some time to be alone and see what you discover.

I CAN COPE WITH BEING ALONE

Acceptance of Others

Lord, try as I might I just don't understand some of these young sistahs today. Maybe I'm just from the old school, but these young womens dat'n each other, marry'n men out the race, let'n theyselves be called foul names, I just don't understand it at all. But I guess if they happy with they lives I don't have to worry. I can just leave it alone, they still my sistahs and I'ma pray for them 'cause God loves us all.

—Mabel

Hip-hop, rap, purple hair, tattoos all over the body, pierced everything! No, I don't understand it, but my parents and grandparents didn't understand the changes that took place during my generation. We don't have to approve of or judge that which we don't understand, we just have to be willing to accept that others have the right to express their non-violent freedoms in a manner that gives them what we've all struggled for in our lifetime—the right to make choices.

I CAN ACCEPT WHAT I
DON'T UNDERSTAND

III

In Sickness and Health

"I'm sick and tired of being sick and tired."

—Fannie Lou Hamer

I heard Fannie Lou Hamer's famous remark for the first time in 1986 when the founder and chairperson of the National Black Women's Health Project, Byllye Avery, spoke at a conference in Seattle, Washington. Byllye Avery's talk on the political, medical, and personal issues that surround our health care inspired me to become a member of the Health Project. I became aware that because we've always been stereotyped and portrayed as both emotionally and physically strong, and because we've desperately tried to live up to that expectation, there's been little attention paid to the key to our survival—our health. Thanks to Byllye's tireless efforts we're starting to pay individual attention and bring national observance to what we need most

in our daily efforts to be "strong" Black women. The quotes in this section are from girlfriends who are starting to pay attention.

 # Personal Power

Not very often, but every now and then I wake up in the morn'n with a smile on my face. It's as if the Lord touched me with his hand and brought me back to life after a hard day's night. Just one of these days can get me through a month of weary Sundays. Girl, I'm tell'n you, on a day like this I can feel the power to heal run'n through my bones clear from my head to my toes. I feel whole, happy, and right with the world. I used to wonder what all them white women was talk'n about when they talked about personal power, but honey, now I know, 'cause on my good days, a whole lot of personal power is pump'n through these bones.

—Dottie

Take a moment, find a quiet place, sit down, and get comfortable. Close your eyes and take three deep breaths. Take the air in through your nose with your mouth closed, then slowly exhale through your mouth. Feel your body relaxing. Keeping your eyes closed, notice your heart beating, listen to the steady rhythm of your heart pumping blood, energy, life, and power all through your body. This exercise takes about fifteen minutes, and if you do

it twice a day it's guaranteed to refresh you and to put you in touch with a sense of your own empowerment.

THERE IS NO PERSONAL POWER
GREATER THAN MY OWN

 # Being Okay

Sometimes folks just get on my nerve always say'n I should be happy about this or that. It's just like I want to tell'm to back off, I'm not happy right now and it ain't no sin. There's a lot of hard stuff go'n down in my life right now and it ain't all about happiness. Anyway not being happy don't mean I'm not alright, cause most of the time I'm doing okay, and if doing okay is all I can manage for right now that's fine.

—LaShawn

This young sister has a very good point—sometimes being okay is all we can manage. I have a collection of what I call "All the Great American Myths." Everybody Is Expected to be Happy heads the list, and unfortunately reality isn't a part of the many items on the list, including the reality of not always feeling and being happy. Sometimes we have things going on in our lives that block our ability to enjoy life at its best. All of us cope the best way we know how, and that includes being okay. Remember the opposite of happiness is not necessarily unhappiness, it can be okay.

I'M DOING OKAY FOR RIGHT NOW

☕ Having Faith

Sometimes I get so tired till my bones ache. I do it all today, just so's I can do it all over again tomorrow. I won't lie to ya, I'm always tempted to ask the good Lord why—but then I know why, 'cause the Lord only asks that we do one thing and that one thing is to step out on faith. And if I ain't got nothin' else I got enough faith to step out on.

—Della

We may lose our way many times in this life, but as long as we have faith we'll be alright.

I CAN STEP OUT ON FAITH

 # God

Child, I respect God, dogs, and the dark in that order, 'cause the last two scare me and only God can protect me. Now I can do my best to avoid dogs, and you won't catch me in the dark by myself, but I don't worry about God, 'cause God is everywhere.

—Anne

When it comes to having a spiritual presence in our lives, I believe that it doesn't matter how we choose to identify, address, or worship that presence. The important thing is that we know and believe that there is always a spiritual presence with and within us.

GOD WILL ALWAYS BE WITH ME

 *Dieting*

My friend told me 'bout this stuff you can drink. . . .

—Penny

I'm very concerned about our obsession with weight. We're underweight, overweight, and going out of our minds trying to be the fashionable weight. Eating disorders are serious and they can not only endanger our health, they can cause death. If you're concerned with how or what you're eating, please see a doctor, don't follow the current diet fads.

I CAN MAKE SAFE FOOD CHOICES

 *Exercise*

Honey, I've got to start do'n some serious work'n out, 'cause I used to be able to pinch an inch, and these days I can fold a roll.

—Micki

Okay, I'll fess up, I recently added walking shoes to my ever growing shoe collection, and I've discovered that there's a reason for the word "sweat" in sweat clothes. Since I've been a member of the National Black Women's Health Project I've become a lot more invested in my health as a Black woman. Through the project I've learned that physical exercise not only helps me to look my best, it helps me to mentally feel my best. So c'mon, girlfriends, let's bust some sweat together.

I'M WILLING TO EXERCISE TO KEEP
MY BODY AND MIND IN SHAPE

 # Hair

The only statement I want my hair to make is, It's gone!

—Jolene

Hair is much too precious in our community. We become hypnotized by it, how much we have or don't have, is it swing straight or too nappy, is it real or weaved, what's political or conservative. I've seen folks stop speaking over hair, and more than one hairdresser has been hauled into court about it. I wonder what would happen if we felt the same way about what was underneath our hair?

I'M MORE THAN MY HAIR

 # Age

My mama always told me not to worry about my age, 'cause good Black don't crack.

—Bessie

Every year on my birthday my mother reminds me that I'm almost grown. According to Momi my gray hairs and few wrinkles don't mean a thing—I'll always be her child. "When will I be grown?" I ask Momi with each passing year, and her responses never fail to make me laugh: "When you get as old as me, kid, when you get as old as me."

I CAN AGE WITH GRACE

 # Color

The blacker the berry . . .   —Old folk saying

This is such a tired subject, but sad to say some of us refuse to give it up. Personally, I think we devote too much time in our community to genetic makeup (pardon the pun). We're all special and shades of color have very little to do with the unique gifts we give to the world. Being fair, dark, or having mixed parentage only has meaning to people who have small minds and very little real meaning in their own lives. The bottom line is that greatness, beauty, and quality don't have color, and you possess all three.

I'M MORE THAN SKIN COLOR

 *Violence*

Girl, I'm tell'n you this—violence amongst ourselves has got to cease.

—Maxie

I agree.

THERE IS NO ROOM IN MY LIFE
FOR VIOLENCE

 Addiction

I used drugs and alcohol to cover my hurt and pain. My recovery has been hard, but I'm stick'n with it like they say, one day at a time. I ask my higher power for the courage to stay straight and sober every day, and so far I've been blessed. I ain't go'n lie, it's a struggle 'cause this mess is strong in the streets where I live. I feel blessed 'cause my family is help'n me get through this, I have their love and support. Mama, Daddy, and the kids are help'n me grow strong, and with their love and my program I'm learn'n how to love and believe in myself.

—Vy

Dangerous habits, those habits that lead to addiction, aren't accidents but habits acquired for immediate relief from the pains and pressures in our lives. We want and need relief from the many demands that are placed on us daily, but please be aware that dangerous habits can only offer us an illusion of relief.

I HAVE THE COURAGE TO OVERCOME
MY ADDICTION

I HAVE THE COURAGE TO STRUGGLE
THROUGH THIS

 # Stress

Are you dealing with any stressful situations right now?

—my doctor

I went in to see my doctor last week. It seems that my eczema has been on the warpath lately and no matter what I do I just can't seem to get it under control. My doctor's question made me think, Yes! There had been a few stressful moments: a computer breakdown, major house remodel, and a few minor things at work, but I had everything under control, or so I thought.

Stress is the invisible sneaky demon; it never tells you when or how it's going to present itself, it just shows up, very much the uninvited guest. Like most of us, I don't really think about how stressful a situation is, I just do what needs to be done. That's where our bodies enter the picture, because stress shows up in our bodies—in my case my skin. I would love to do away with stress altogether, but since that's not possible, the next best thing would be to take really good care of our bodies, so when we do have a stress attack, at least we'll be in shape for it.

I CAN PREPARE MYSELF TO
HANDLE STRESS

 # Grief

I know I'll get through this but Lord it sure does hurt. It's been two years, but sometimes I cry like it was yesterday. I guess the feel'n you carry from losing somebody you love just don't get old no matter when it happens.

—Clovis

The pain we carry when someone close to us dies can be staggering, and we can and often do feel helpless in knowing how to cope. Please remember that while the pain may never truly go away it does lessen with time.

MY GRIEF DOESN'T HAVE
A TIME LINE

 *Tears*

There's only two times when people are gonna see me cry: when I'm ready to fight, and if I get hurt real bad and can't help myself. I don't like to cry 'cause it's a sign of weakness.

—Gloria

We've been raised in a culture that denies us the value of experiencing our sadness. I believe that tears are a sign of release. Crying is a way of letting go, moving forward out of the dark recesses of our pain and grief. Have you ever noticed how much better you feel after a good cry? Tears are a natural part of our emotional cleansing system and they promote our ability to heal.

MY TEARS ARE PART OF
MY STRENGTH

 # Happiness

*Sistahs are always blow'n me out say'n that I'm not
real 'cause I'm always so cheerful and happy. At first I
got worried 'cause I thought I was miss'n somethin'. But
then I just figured this is the way I am, so be it. I finally
told my friends hey, you all can walk around under a
cloud of gloom and doom if you want to, but that ain't
the way I work, so if you don't like the train I'm on just
ride on through, 'cause I'ma be me.*

—Mary Rose

This sister's statement really took me by surprise,
because it never occured to me that people would be
upset over another person's happiness. True, there's a
lot of ugly stuff happening in the world, but not everyone chooses to focus on the ugliness. We can, like
this sister, choose how we're going to view our world.

I CHOOSE TO BE HAPPY IN MY LIFE

 *Healing*

When I think back on it, there's been a lot of hurt in my life. I was abused as a child and I'm just now git'n out of an abusive marriage. I got a lot of heal'n to do, but that's okay. I made a vow 'fore God to myself that so long as I got one breath in my body I'm gonna put the past in the good Lord's hands and take care of myself for the present. That's all I got to say.

—Ada

The art of emotional healing is a very individual process aside from one common element—time. Sometimes our hurts can be so strong and painful that it's difficult to imagine our survival, but we do survive and we do go on. With each new day we move toward a place of healing the pain we've suffered. I'm not talking about forgetting, because we may never forget what caused our hurt. But with time we do have the power to emotionally move away from whatever it was that hurt us. If you give yourself nothing else, please give yourself all the time you need to heal.

I HEAL MY PAST BY LIVING IN THE
PRESENT AND GIVING MYSELF TIME

 # *Depression*

Sometimes I just get in these moods where it seems like everything just gets on my last nerve. If you look at me wrong I'm ready to jump down your throat. It's like I'm so edgy until I want to climb out my skin and nothing seems to make much sense. My friend Letha said I might be depressed, but I don't think I'm crazy.

—Ruby

Being depressed is not being crazy. We all experience depression from time to time, it's almost a fact of life. When we have too much stress in our lives we get overwhelmed, and when we're overwhelmed our regular emotional responses shut down. In the clinical field, depression is known as a mood disorder, which simply means that our emotional mood is or has been down for a period of time. Sometimes people can move through a period of depression without professional help. However, if the depressed mood lasts for more than a two-week time span, it would be wise to seek professional assistance.

I CAN GET THROUGH THIS
WITH SOME HELP

 *Relaxation*

I get up every morning at 5:30 and hit the bed every night at 11:00 and I can't really call any of that time my own. It seems like I'm tired 365, 24, 7, with no time off for good behavior. My doctor says I got to relax more if I want my blood pressure to come down, but where's the time gonna come from?

—Shirley

Too much to do and too little time, we've all been there; but, hey, when it's a question of our health, it's time to put ourselves in the mix and make our needs a priority. Twenty minutes out of every day is a small price to pay when it could mean a lifetime of good health. Do yourself a favor, girlfriend, build some time into your busy schedule to relax—you've earned it.

I'VE EARNED THE RIGHT TO RELAX

Personal Health

I never in a million years would have believed I'd get breast cancer. I thought I was doing everything right, but maybe I missed something. The doctor says I'm lucky 'cause they caught it in time, so I have a chance at full recovery. But I don't feel very lucky right about now.

—Chris

Personally I hate being sick. I know my weaknesses and my strengths and sickness is at the top of my weakness list (no pun intended). Let's face it, sickness means I'm not at my personal best. (Not counting doctor visits, because I'm one of those people who believes in getting medical attention, taking medication—have you noticed the size of some of those pills, they're big enough to choke a horse—and losing time from work. . . . Okay so maybe I can deal with that part.) Actually, I'm making light of a very serious issue, but I've found humor to be healing. I used to believe that my personal illness, mainly my eczema, was some form of curse or punishment from God. But as I learned more about my family health history and about my body I discovered that eczema tends to run in families. I also discovered that while eczema is generally found in children, in rare cases it can last well into adulthood and very often can be

triggered by allergies, stress, and other unknown causes. My point is, my sickness is a part of me, I'm human, and sickness is a human condition. It's neither good nor bad, God didn't curse me, though sometimes when I'm feeling really bad I curse God (my God understands this radical behavior and blesses me anyway). I can do all the *right things* and I will still have outbreaks from time to time. Don't blame yourself or believe that it's God's will, take care of yourself and please seek medical attention.

I AM MORE THAN MY SICKNESS

IV

Over the Back Fence

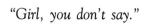

"Girl, you don't say."

My mother and Miss Eleanor, our next-door neighbor in New Jersey, were back fence girlfriends. When Momi wasn't in the house looking after our needs, she was standing at the back fence deep in conversation with Miss Eleanor. Everything was discussed over the back fence by these two unofficial, but highly respected local representatives of Kenwood Avenue. Births, deaths, neighborhood happenings, church socials, and the soaps. Refrains of "No, girl," "Say what?" "Girl, git outta here," and "You don't say" punctuated the air as we kids played in the yard. Any sudden interruptions were greeted with the "look," and trying to chime into their conversation without invitation was greeted with, "Don't you see grown folks talk'n. . . ." This wasn't so much a question as it was a dismissal. If there

were too many interruptions the girlfriend talk ended only to be picked up again later on in the evening shade of the front porch after we had gone to bed.

This section of the book is girlfriend talk that might be heard over the back fence.

Shit Happens, or Control Attack

I went to pay for groceries and found I didn't have my checkbook, the mechanic says he can't find the knock'n sound, and to top it off the shower drain is stopped up and the plumber can't make it till Monday. Lord!! Why me?

—Julia

There are some days when I just want to sit on the curb and let out a moan that can be heard around the world. On days like this I truly believe that in a world where shit happens, it must be my turn to shovel the pile. Recently when I was whining and complaining to a friend who's involved in A.A. (Alcoholics Anonymous), my friend told me to remember that I didn't start it, I can't control it, and I don't have to fix it, or something on that order, and then calmly told me to take one thing at a time. Yes! I had forgotten that I didn't need to have control over every little thing, and it was only when I believed that I needed to be in control that I actually lost control. So once again I've decided to give up control for Lent.

I CAN LET GO OF MY NEED TO CONTROL

 *Hope*

All I can say is there were times when I was ready to give up.

—Flo

As long as there is hope there is a chance that change can happen. I have an imaginary change purse that I keep with me all the time. In my imaginary purse I keep four coins: Hope, Faith, Confidence, and Compassion. My purse and coins are always with me and whenever I find myself in a situation that requires me to spend one of my coins I just pull it out and go for broke. Now over the years I've found that these coins are magic, because they always manage to replace themselves. I think we all have a magic coin when we have hope.

I ALWAYS HAVE HOPE

 # Perfection

I'm not picky, but I do believe if you can't do something right don't do it at all.

—Rose

There are a list of words and definitions that I would love to see taken out of the dictionary and "perfection" heads the list. Trying to be perfect is a setup for failure, because no matter how hard we try, we're going to fall short either in our own minds or someone else's. I read a book not long ago where the author said we should dare to be average. Now that sounds like something I can handle.

I DON'T HAVE TO BE PERFECT

 Success

Lord, honey—I don't know what I can say about being successful. I'm seventy-two years old, the good Lord has blessed me with good health, I've seen all my children grown and on their own, and I got a little bit of money in the bank. That's all I ever prayed for, and I got it, so I guess you could say those things were my success.

—Bertha

Whenever I would tell Mama about something I wanted or wished for she would tell me to be careful what I prayed for because I just might get it. I took Mama's words to heart and these days I only wish, want, and pray for the best, no need of wasting all that hard work on second best. On the serious side of things I think that it's difficult to measure personal success without giving ourselves some type of measurable yardstick. If we're going to measure our success in terms of money, how much money? If it's work, how much and what kind of work? The key to being successful is setting solid goals and then working toward meeting them. Personally, I prefer daily goals: They're smaller and easier to meet and I can see the results when I'm done, which helps me to feel suc-

cessful. I guess if there were an equation for success it would look like this:

Pray for it + Set it + Work like mad to get it = Success.

I CAN OBTAIN MY SUCCESS

 *Hard Work*

There's only one thing on God's green earth that I'll ever beg for, and that's my life. Anything else I get I expect to work my Black fingers to the bone for, and that's my bottom line.

—Lettie

Zoey said I didn't need to include a page on doing hard work, " 'cause Black folks are experts at it." Now of course this girlfriend is right, we sure do know how to punch a time clock. But I think it's one thing to know how to work, and it's something else to enjoy the work we do. Like Lettie, I'm willing to work my fingers to the bone when I believe in what I'm doing. Having a sense of pride in the work we produce helps us to have a sense of pride about ourselves.

I CAN BE PROUD OF THE WORK I DO

Employment

I don't really like the job I have right now, but it's a starting place and it keeps the bills paid. My all-time dream is to start my own travel business. I don't have the money right now but I've been taking business courses at night at the community college, and as soon as I'm finished I'm going to look into raising the capital I'll need to get started.

—Vicki

If you're not where you want to be in terms of employment, what are you willing to do to get there? Take classes, find a mentor, find volunteer work that will enable you to reach your employment goals. Remember, a job is what you have to do, a career is what you want to do.

I WILL WORK TOWARD MY
CAREER CHOICE

 # Money

Mama always told me that a dollar was a Black woman's best friend. Mama says a dollar don't give you no lip, it'll feed you when you're hungry, clothe you when you're cold, and keep the rain off your head. Yes, ma'am, if you treat a dollar right, it multiplies, and if you don't it disappears, but if you got a dollar, you've got a friend for life.

—Flo

I have this love/hate relationship with money. I love it when I have some and hate it when I don't. What can I say, I'm a material girl in a money-run world and I've got my running shoes on. And while I'll admit up front that I don't worship money, it does seem to run a pretty close second. Let's be real— having money allows certain freedoms, like supporting my family, paying my bills (which are too numerous to mention), saving for old age, and doing my all-time favorite—shopping. I'm willing to work hard in order to earn money, and I don't mind sharing what I earn with family, very close friends, and special organizations. I guess I'm saying all this be-

cause money has gotten such a bad rap over the years. Money isn't bad, and having money or wanting it isn't bad either.

MONEY SERVES A USEFUL PURPOSE
IN MY LIFE

 Education

I pass'd by the schoolhouse door even if I didn't go in.

—Annie

I believe that we all possess knowledge, and since we are all individuals the knowledge we possess is individual knowledge. We can enhance our individual knowledge at any given time by: going to school, sharing conversations with others on different subjects, reading books, watching educational programs, going on trips, reading newspapers, listening to tapes, watching others perform tasks, asking questions, attending lectures. . . . As long as we're open to learning there will always be something new for us to learn.

I'M ALWAYS OPEN TO LEARNING
SOMETHING NEW

 *Time*

When I was a little girl I used to think that time went too slow, now I think it goes much too fast.

—Gen

If I were a magic genie I would get rid of all the clocks in the world and develop a system of time that didn't require people to keep track of their lives in seconds, minutes, and hours. We waste so much time worrying about time until we never have the time to do the things that really count.

I HAVE ALL THE TIME I NEED

 # Gossip

Mama always told me that any dog that will bring a bone, will carry a bone. Far as I know Mama ain't lied to me yet. So when sistahs come to me to dish the dirt, I tell'm straight up, don't be drop'n no bones in my back-yard 'cause I don't aim to keep'm.

—Bess

Have you ever noticed that gossip is never good news? Frankly I hear enough depressing and bad news via the daily media to fill a lifetime quota so I'm not really interested in hearing hurtful or bad secondhand news. If we're going to talk about each other, let's talk openly about the good stuff.

I DON'T NEED GOSSIP IN MY LIFE

 # *Opinions*

I don't care what nobody say, I think the brother was set up.

—Connie

I love opinions; almost everybody has one. And most of us, including myself, are generally pretty generous when it comes to sharing our opinions. But the very best thing about opinions is that they allow us to feel right about something. We may end up being wrong when all the facts come to light, that is if the facts exist. Facts really don't matter in this, 'cause we felt right about our opinions and that's all that counts.

MY OPINION COUNTS

 # *Apologizing*

I don't know why she got so mad, she should've known I didn't mean it.

—Frankie

How many times have we let others walk away with hurt feelings when an apology was in order? Mama used to tell us kids, "Say'n I'm sorry won't cost you one red cent"—and you and I know Mama's right. So let's put our pride in our pocket and keep our relationships with others intact.

I CAN APOLOGIZE WHEN I'M WRONG

 *Attitude*

Girl, don't mess with her, she got up with her habits on this morn'n.

—Karen

We sisters have some powerful attitude. I get so tickled sometimes when I hear a white sister talking about her last mood swing or PMS, 'cause where I grew up those same symptoms of behavior would be and still are considered "attitude." But I love the fact that we have attitude, because let's face it, there are times when we need to tell the world to back up and git out our faces—and attitude lets us do it without making excuses. Attitude has allowed many of us to take that extra step to go one more mile when the going got tough, so in my book attitude is alright with me.

MY ATTITUDE IS A SURVIVAL TOOL

 Forgiveness

It's up to her. I'll speak if she speaks, I didn't start this mess.

—JoAnn

Sometimes we make life so hard for ourselves. I recently saw a bumper sticker that said DON'T SWEAT THE SMALL STUFF. IT'S ALL SMALL STUFF. Holding a grudge takes a lot of emotional energy which is generally not to our benefit. When we hold a grudge, we're holding a hurtful part of the past that keeps us from being fully in the present. When we give ourselves permission to be forgiving, we free up energy, and that energy allows us to get on with our lives.

I'M WILLING TO FORGIVE

 *Trust*

> My friends tell me I'm cold-blooded 'cause I don't trust nobody. But, hey, I been there and let me tell you git'n burned ain't my idea of fun—okay?
>
> —Sharon

It's hard to trust others when we've been hurt in the past. This is especially true if the someone who betrayed our trust was close to us in a personal way. I think that sometimes we forget just how valuable trust really is in our lives. I was taught that one's trust was a sacred bond that once broken could never be redeemed. As an adult I no longer believe that a broken trust can't be mended, depending on the circumstances, of course. But it's my duty to tell others the conditions for earning or re-earning my trust.

I CAN LET PEOPLE EARN MY TRUST

 # Kindness

It really burns me up when folks walk down the street and don't speak. It don't hurt nothing and nobody to offer a hello.

—Vonda

When we show ourselves a little bit of kindness, it makes it easier to offer it to others.

I'M WILLING TO SHOW KINDNESS
TO MYSELF AND OTHERS

 # Feelings

My daughter wants me to see a counselor 'cause she says I don't show my feelings.

—Nettie

We all have feelings, but depending on where and how we were raised it wasn't always safe to visibly show what we were thinking or feeling. In order to express our emotions openly we have to be comfortable and believe that we're not going to be judged or punished in some way for revealing ourselves. Not expressing how we feel doesn't mean we don't have feelings—it just means that we don't feel safe at that given time.

MY FEELINGS ARE IMPORTANT

 # Rap Music

Kelvin and his friends was at the house the other night play'n tapes and some of the stuff they was listenin' to made me so mad.

—Bobbie

I'm not going to lie, some song lyrics are just plain disgusting, especially the references to women, and I'm not going to single out rap music as the only bad guy here. The other night I was listening to some old blues records and the references to women in some of those songs made rap music look downright tame. I don't believe in censorship, but in my house I believe in equal shared listening time. Just as my son introduced me to rap I introduced him to Sweet Honey in the Rock, Rachel Bagby, and some of my other favorites. I have to admit I like some of his music, and I've heard him humming one of Sweet Honey's songs as he was cleaning up the kitchen.

I'M WILLING TO LOOK AT
BOTH SIDES OF AN ISSUE

 # *Mistakes*

I hate it when I screw somethin' up. I gave this lady the wrong change yesterday and she was pretty nice about it and all. But it was like, oh wow, how could I be so stupid.

—Raylene

We really do beat ourselves up over making mistakes. I've found more sisters nailed to crosses of their own making just because they've made a mistake. We're not stupid when we make mistakes, we're tired, so maybe the mistake is our minds' way of saying, Lighten up, girlfriend.

I CAN FORGIVE MYSELF FOR
MAKING MISTAKES

 # Assertiveness

Everybody says that I'm too direct, too out there. I can't help it, that's just the way I am. I speak my mind.

—Willie

Being assertive can be a real gift, as long as it's used in a positive way. Being assertive means that we feel confident and positive about ourselves and what we are doing, or saying. When we feel good about ourselves it's easy to assert ourselves in a confident manner.

MY ASSERTIVENESS IS
A POSITIVE GIFT

 # *Sensitivity*

Kenny is all the time say'n that I'm too sensitive, then when I lay him out about somethin' he says I'm too cold.

—Tangie

Everybody has a sensitive, soft side. It's that part of ourselves that allows us to express our tenderness and love for people and things that we enjoy. I'm always highly suspicious of those who try to use our sensitivity as a weapon against us. What are they telling us, that we shouldn't be tender and caring or that our show of affection makes them uncomfortable? Being sensitive is an important part of being human.

I'M PROUD OF MY SENSITIVITY

 *Decisions*

Sometimes I get so caught up in try'n to make up my mind, til' I forget what I was try'n to make up my mind about.

—Maxie

Just for the record, there is no such thing as a right or wrong decision. When you get right down to the wire any decision you make is the best decision for you at that moment.

I CAN MAKE DECISIONS

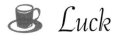 # *Luck*

I play the lottery every week, 'cause I figure my number's got to come up sometime.

—Jackie

Luck is nice when it happens, but it's not something that we can count on regularly.

PART OF MY LUCK IS
HARD WORK

 *Abundance*

Girl! What in the world are you gonna do with all them shoes?

—Momi

I love shoes, and I have a lot of them. No particular reason, I see a pair—it doesn't matter where, Kmart to Saks—I like them, I buy them. There's no doubt about it, I have an abundance of shoes. Momi says that I don't need all those shoes, but she doesn't realize that physical need has very little to do with it. I even walk around barefoot when I'm home. I like shoes, I have shoes, and it feels good. We all need an abundance of good things in our lives—mine just happens to be shoes.

I CAN ENJOY ABUNDANCE
IN MY LIFE

Waiting for Change

I saw on the news where this high school in Alabama was burned down and when this Black news reporter tried to get the story, he was beat up and called names by the white school principal. I keep want'n to believe things have changed but I guess not.

—Ronnie

Things have changed: We have better laws on the books, and more visible Black leadership. Unfortunately, better laws and visible Black leadership don't change people's attitudes. The work that we did in the sixties and seventies is a continuous process and we can't believe that the work we've done was for nothing. There are always going to be struggles, but our fighting has made us stronger.

CHANGE IS A CONTINUOUS PROCESS

 *Spirituality*

I was raised in the church, and I still go every Sunday, but I don't know, it just seems like . . .

—Francis

Feeling close to God isn't a church thing, feeling close to God is a personal thing. Church is a place of fellowship and communal worship, but sometimes we need private time with God and that's hard to get when we're surrounded by others. We have to remember that God lives within us, and we always have access to God's ear. So don't wait for Sundays.

I WILL ALWAYS BE IN THE
PRESENCE OF GOD

 # Prayers

I'm praying for ya. —Dee

I was telling a close friend recently that while I don't consider myself a religious person I do tend to find a great deal of comfort in prayer. My friend, who didn't seem to find my remark at all unusual, remarked that praying wasn't about religion, but more about having faith. My friend is right, it doesn't matter who or what we believe in. Prayer confirms our sense of faith and belief that things can get better, that we'll survive whatever has been put before us.

I HAVE FAITH IN PRAYER

 # Affirmation

Peace be still. —Nona

I heard this sister say this affirmation after a support-group meeting. When I asked her about it she said that when she needed comforting she would say it over and over to herself.

I love affirmations; I think of them as personal prayers to myself for myself. Just as we believe and pray to our higher power, we can believe and pray to ourselves. Doing one doesn't discount the other—affirmations and prayers complement each other. Affirmations allow us to stay in touch with ourselves on a daily basis and give us a way to check in and boost our emotional energy. Use affirmations to affirm your belief in yourself.

I CAN AFFIRM MY BELIEF IN MYSELF

 *Being Blessed*

I'm so blessed. . . .   —Tina

I've heard this sentiment (it's more than a statement) from sisters everywhere and it's so true. We manage through thick and thin to take that extra step, to go that extra mile. We accomplish the impossible and achieve the unbelievable and through it all we are blessed. We have always been blessed, and will remain so.

I AM SO BLESSED

I KNOW I'M A BEAUTIFUL BLACK/
AFRICAN-AMERICAN WOMAN BECAUSE

MY SELF-CARE FOR TODAY WILL BE

I LOVE MYSELF WHEN I

MY ONE GOAL FOR TODAY IS

I CAN SHOW OTHER SISTERS SUPPORT BY

I'M PROUD OF

I FEEL EMPOWERED WHEN I

I HAVE THE SUPPORT OF

MY PERSONAL AFFIRMATION IS

I AM BLESSED BECAUSE

· A NOTE ON THE TYPE ·

The typeface used in this book is a version of Goudy
(Old Style), originally designed by Frederick W. Goudy
(1865–1947), perhaps the best known and certainly one of
the most prolific of American type designers, who created
over a hundred typefaces—the actual number is unknown
because a 1939 fire destroyed many of his drawings and
"matrices" (molds from which type is cast). Initially a
calligrapher, rather than a type cutter or printer, he rep-
resented a new breed of designer made possible by late-
nineteenth-century technological advances; later on, in
order to maintain artistic control, he supervised the produc-
tion of matrices himself. He was also a tireless promoter of
wider awareness of type, with the paradoxical result that
the distinctive style of his influential output tends to be as-
sociated with his period and, though still a model of taste,
can now seem somewhat dated.